FRACTURED HEART, Mended Soul

A COLLECTION OF POETRY AND PROSE ON THE SUBJECTS OF...

HEARTBREAK,
LOVE,
HEALING,

&

SOUL LESSONS

By Samantha Woodbeck

Fractured Heart, Mended Soul

Copyright © 2022 Samantha Woodbeck

All rights reserved.

ISBN:9798833678725

This book, or any portion thereof, may not be reproduced or used in any manner whatsoever without the express written permission of the publisher, except for the use of brief quotations in a book review.

Cover Photo used from https://burst.shopify.com/

Artist: Arif Amin

Find me on Instagram and Facebook

@Soul_Spilled_Sentiments

DEDICATION

This book is dedicated to all of the people who have reached out, opened up their hearts, and trusted me with their stories.

To the heartbroken, the lost.

To all the inner children who have overcome impossible obstacles, or who are still in the process of healing.

To the loved, the found.

May you always take the lessons you learn along the way and strive towards your soul's highest good.

To the healed and healers. Thank you.
Keep lighting the way.

Love, ♥
Samantha

Fractured Heart, Mended Soul

I FIND MYSELF HEALING
IN SCARS STITCHED
TOGETHER
BETWEEN A FRACTURED
HEART AND MENDED
SOUL...

SPILLED ONTO
THESE PAGES
IN DIFFERENT PARTS,

BOUND TOGETHER,

AND
ULTIMATELY...

MAKING ME
WHOLE.

Fractured Heart, Mended Soul

CONTENTS

Part. 1 Heartbreak - 14

Tired Reality - 15

Eternally Speaking - 16

Love as a Lethal Weapon - 17

Final Resting Place - 18

Oceans Apart - 19

Drowning Inevitably - 20

Within These Walls - 21

Across Lifetimes - 22

From The Inside - 23

Strings Attached - 24

Ashes - 25

Blank Pages - 26

Neverland - 27

Wins and Losses - 28

Save Me (From Myself) - 29

Emotional Asphyxiation - 30

Swallowing Truth - 31

Self-Induced Amnesia - 32

Ricochet - 33

Space Between - 34

Risked and Lost - 35

Selectively Illiterate - 36

Sweet Nothings - 37

Better Luck Next Time - 38

Clear as Crimson - 39

Battle Cry - 40

Triggered - 41

Haunted - 42

Silent Scars - 43

Battleground - 44

Different Worlds - 45

Under The Influence - 46

Caged In - 47

Lost at Sea (In My Soul) - 48

Fighting the Familiar - 49

Rhythmic Release - 50

Love's Logic - 51

Bittersweet Release - 52

Truth Dipped in Poison - 53

Ripped Open - 54

Lying Lullabies - 55

Suicide Love - 56

Part 2. Love - 57

Rising Above Reason - 58

Written Between Our Souls - 59

Chamber Walls - 60

All Things Warm - 61

Everything - 62

Kiss Me - 63

Poetic Love - 64

Timeless Love - 65

Complicated - 66

Wrapped Up in Your Love - 67

Light In My Darkness - 68

No Place Like Home - 69

Uninterrupted Space - 70

Trapped, But Free - 71

Reflections - 72

Electricity - 73

Embedded - 74

You - 75

Part 3. Healing and Soul Lessons - 76

It Hurts - 77

Shadow Work - 78

Saving Ourselves - 79

Undone - 80

Anomaly - 81

Brighter Days - 82

The Light Within - 83

Peace Amongst Demons - 84

The Calm in My Storm - 85

Growing Pains - 86

The Space Between - 87

Gone - 88

Weeds and Wishes - 89

Shaped Soul - 90

Spiritual Journey - 91

Still Alive - 92

Caged - 93

Dead End - 94

Poetry and Pain - 95

Held - 96

Love and Logic - 97

Lost in Translation - 98

Enslaved, But Saved - 99

The Ocean in My Bones - 100

Free to Fly - 101

Layered in Light - 102

Keeper of Darkness - 103

Unbreakable - 104

Set Free - 105

Writing Myself Well - 106

Written Rampage - 107

Hungry For Love - 108

Thank You - 110

Wholly Healing - 111

Strengthening My Soul - 112

Written Remedy - 113

Inner Work - 114

Never Will Be - 115

Lightworkers - 116

No One Believed Me - 117

Shaping My Soul - 118

Crossroad - 119

Beautiful Darkness - 120

Don't Get Me Wrong - 121

Misaligned - 122

Submerged in Self-Reflection - 123

War Zone - 124

Crying Words - 125

Wishing You Well - 126

Needed Most - 127

Finally Free - 128

Feeling The Fall - 129

Unfolded - 130

Breaking to Become - 131

Seeds of Hope - 132

Aligned - 133

Meant to Stay - 134

Home - 135

More - 136

Forget - 137

Worlds Apart - 138

Sacred Sounds - 139

The Hope - 140

Highest Good - 141

Learning to Listen - 142

The Journey - 143

Leaving Us Raw - 144

Wrong and Right - 145

Some of Us - 146

Lifetimes of Lessons - 147

The Shift - 148

Born Into Darkness - 149

The Way Home - 150

Warrior Spirit - 151

My Dear Sweet Child - 152

Silence of My Soul - 153

Neville Goddard Quote - 154

About the Author - 155

Fractured Heart, Mended Soul

Heartbreak

Tired Reality

I couldn't sleep again.
I woke up with a flood of heartbreak poems
I need to write,
but can't bring myself to read.
Sometimes I wish I could edit myself out of my own story...
Change the reality
and for once
set my heart free.

Eternally Speaking

In a world full of unlimited words,

silence can be a cure

or an enemy.

Words can be wisdom,

the weapon, or the remedy.

Like ingredients in a spell,

choose them carefully and methodically.

They hold so much power,

healing and hurting...

Endlessly

and

magically.

Love as a Lethal Weapon

All is fair in *love* and **war**.
So they say.
You've heard it all before.
But the lines,
they *blur*.
And I can't tell whether I'm falling
or fighting,
living or dying.
My heart became the battleground;
unreconciled,
down to the core.
I pray for a peace treaty with my mind,
as you've turned combat into an art form.
Not sure if the bloodshed is evidence of
victory or surrender;
a loss or a gain…
When even enemies sacrifice *love* as a
lethal weapon,
inflicting pain and
trapping you…

With nothing left but **scars**
as remains.

Final Resting Place

Hollow heart,
like an empty grave.
Carved with my own hands,
but the headstone bears your name.
My raw fingertips trace each one of your letters leaving bloodstains.
You're no longer here, but still your presence remains.
My body has become a cemetery filled with remorse as memories echo through my chamber walls.
Broken promises play on repeat,
like a ghost haunting these abandoned halls.
One after another I want to bury them alive,
but my scars will never let me forget.
My love for you runs deep,
but this deathbed is overflowing with regret.
My wounds continue to bleed internally,
filling every available space.
I'm flooded with your demons,
and how I wish my soul wasn't their final
resting place.

Oceans Apart

You let me scratch the surface,
but wouldn't allow me to swim beneath the waves.

No wonder I was left to

D
R
O
W
N

in such a shallow soul of a grave.

Drowning Inevitably

I have bruises you can't see,
as my heart bleeds internally.
Constantly
inside of me.
All the pain trapped deep within,
hidden wounds trapped under my skin.
Scars that have never been fully healed.
Held hostage,
but never revealed.
Below the surface.
Eternally.
Drowning me
inevitably.

Within These Walls

We occupy these same four walls,
but live in different worlds.
Day after day
we are physically here
but emotionally far away.
We share this place,
night after night,
but fill it with empty space.
Appearing close
when in reality we're so far.
The internal void only grows.
Our detached souls,
and disconnected hearts
meander through these empty halls.
We're dying inside while living worlds apart,
and still trapped within these lonely walls.

Across Lifetimes

I tried so hard to cut you out of my heart.
Attempting in vain
time after time
falling apart
in pieces again.
This heart of mine
it's relentless it seems,
and the blood;
it just continues to pour.
For it still beats across lifetimes,
shattered and scarred,
in many parts,
completely detached...
But forever in sync
with yours.

From The Inside

Your memories eat away at me like acid from the inside.

Slowly dissolving so much that's unseen from deep within where it tries to hide. They secretly devour me without leaving a trace, as no one can see it through the forced smile on my face.

Looking at me, you'd never know how hard I fight to camouflage your demons, blending them in with my own.

My inner turmoil is now reaping all the collateral damage you've meticulously sown.

Strings Attached

I was so wrapped up in the threads of you...

Strings attached
soul tied
heart knotted
mind tangled.

That I lost all awareness of my own
unraveling.
You let me go,
but somehow
I was still
completely
strangled.

Ashes

There was so much beauty hidden in these ashes.

You just refused to look through the smoke to see it.

Blank Pages

I haven't let myself write in a while.

It's because I'm trying to be strong,

 but really I'm just in denial.

Every poem starts out with,

"I miss you so damn much it hurts...."

And then I stop myself and try to save face,

since my heart has already gone missing.

But I can't stop missing you.

So I sit here with blank pages and a soul full of all the things

I feel...

But won't let myself say.

Neverland

I try to think happy thoughts, honestly I do…

But they all seem to have flown away. Vanished.
Just like you.

Are they in Neverland, not aging and
unchanging like the lost boys?

Where time stands still and yesterdays blend into endless
tomorrows?

Where no one grows up and there aren't any sorrows?

All I know is I'm here, and they're somewhere far.

Wherever they may be, I'm guessing they're right
where you are.

In some far off world.

Leaving me with only sadness, without you, and

a very lost girl.

Wins and Losses

You kept me like a trophy,

but I felt like more of a white flag.

The paradox of victory and surrender.

Save Me (From Myself)

Save me
From making that age old mistake.
For falling in the trap I finally crawled out of.
Save me from believing the lies.
From getting lost in his eyes.
From binding my soul
and following my heart,
while ignoring my brain.
Save me from myself
When I doubt everything I said
in an attempt to be strong and move on.
Save me from falling in love
with him all over again,
Opening up old wounds
now bleeding through my pen.
I thought I was healed,
but I was so wrong.
How could I fool myself
for so long?

Emotional Asphyxiation

I still feel parts of you lingering in the depths of my lungs every time I breathe in.
I hesitate to exhale completely and risk giving up what little of you I have left.
Afraid to choke.
I draw you in.
I hold my breath and let the tears flow.
Grasping onto what's been keeping me alive all this time.
You've been my lifeline.
Gasping now.
I begin to run out of air.
I inhale the truth, but refuse to let it out.
I'd rather suffocate for lack of oxygen,
than watch my soul surrender you with the CO_2 and suffer the emotional asphyxiation,
of losing what's left of you.

Swallowing Truth

All the tears are gone.

The aftertaste of regret still lingers
in the back of my throat.

I choke down the harsh truth last,
in hopes that I don't vomit it back up again

Self Induced Amnesia

It's going to hurt, but it's the only way. I'm going to carve out every last bit of you that even dares to stay. You cannot remain. No anesthesia. I need to feel the pain. I want nothing left. Not even memories.
Self induced amnesia.
Nothing that triggers my heart to recognize you. Overdosed truth serum swallowed in force fed bittersweet reality. Choked down. I want to be as empty of you as your heart was before it siphoned my soul, leaving me void of all hope, heartbroken, as you robbed me to make yourself feel whole. You only love me when you're empty, and it's beyond clear now. You set my heart on fire to keep yourself warm, never even noticing the collateral damage of scars I end up with from the flames of hell you throw.

Ricochet

Stop using my love as a weapon to trap me.

It **ricochets** off you so hard that it *cuts* me every time.

Space Between

I didn't think you'd be so quick to burn the bridge you just rebuilt.

But here I am and there you are, with nothing but smoke, space, and a river running through us.

Broken board remnants and lingering dust fall into the water.

Without ceasing, the current rushes by taking all the evidence of you and me.

My only hope now is it washes my soul clean and heals every last internal scar you made, but can't see.

Risked and Lost

It's the apology I'll never get.

Constant reminders of past regret.

Pulsing through me so I won't forget.

My soul is scarred and forever in debt.

I risked it all on you...

And still lost my heart in love's bet.

Selectively Illiterate

You and I really aren't that much different.

It's just that I choose to wear my words on the outside...

And you pretend not to know how to **read.**

Sweet Nothings

Our love was like a short-lived daydream trapped between recurring nightmares.

I couldn't wake up and you kept slipping me sleeping pills between kisses under your tongue.

Better Luck Next Time

Every time you come back I start planning the farewell party and rehearsing my goodbye lines. You approach me with false promises, that I somehow believe every single time. Your departure is inevitable, but it's a sacrifice I make. Really more of a mistake. A lesson I never learn, even though I know all the answers ahead of time. You win a game I don't like to play as my heart breaks and I lose my mind thinking (but knowing better) better luck next time.

Clear as Crimson

My heart poured out.
Every last drop.
Spilled an entire mess all over the floor
in the shape of you.

I see it now for what it is.
A beautiful illusion.
A sad delusion of my injured soul.
My own unraveling.
Still, somehow you remain whole.

It was my brutal undoing and you just watched,
silently unaffected.
My fragile heart wounded as I bled out
completely dry.
Everything neglected and left wondering why.

It's all so crimson clear now except…

Were you the one holding the knife,

or was I?

Battle Cry

I've laid aside
all the memories
rendering you unrecognizable
in my mind.
At least I try to
make you hard to find.
But my heart still beats,
for you it seems.
I see you in everything,
and feel it constantly.
Silent thunderstorms rage in me,
and when it rains it absolutely pours.
I hear it echo everywhere...

This battle cry of my soul
in a never ending war with yours.

Triggered

Your silence is a lethal weapon,
and I'm tired of being target practice.
Are you tone deaf to love or just ignore me out of malice?
You have perfect aim and choose to shoot around the outer
edges of my heart. Precisely carved, but not torn out.
Enough collateral damage to keep me alive. Barely
breathing, heart still beating,
while so much of me has already died.
The quietness grows so intense. I feel it echoing; the bullets
and the blasts. My ears are ringing, needing to stop the
bleeding fast.
Yet, you refuse to say a single word,
missing the bullseye at the center of it all.
The last fatal shot's sound could open the lingering wound
where healing could start, and closure could finally be
found. I'm done fighting you in this one-sided war...
Every time you pull the muted trigger, it cuts me down to
my soul's core.

Haunted

You were the rude awakening to my trauma-induced slumber.

Now all I can do is hope to dream and find some peace between the living and the deceased.

The harsh reality of being awake, and the horror of falling into another deep sleep.

My soul, stuck in this trance, has long since departed, but you're a living, breathing ghost.

I'm stuck between two nightmares,
and you're haunting me in both.

Silent Scars

You cut me with such careful precision,
like a gifted surgeon or perhaps
a skilled murderer.
Leaving no evidence of the incision,
my tears were the only sutures.
I healed with no external scars,
but there was still so much pain.
You left poison memories
under the surface.
Now toxicity runs rampantly
through my veins.

Battleground

It was unfair
for me to chase after something
that wasn't anchored down.
Always running around
losing ground,
becoming unhinged.
Chasing your love
that wasn't able
to be found.
All the while
losing myself,
piece by piece
wounded and scarred;
a casualty
left alone.
Bleeding words
on love's battleground.

Different Worlds

Your silence spoke louder than anything you could have said.

You played with my heart and messed with my head. I found so much quiet validation,
in your absolute nothingness, that was the final confirmation.
Zero communication.
You only loved me when you felt lonely,
siphoning my soul while using my body.
I had so much to say, but now I couldn't care less.
You've done absolutely nothing for my heart over the years,
except cause unnecessary stress.
It's not that I'll ever run out of words...

But you'll never understand them,
because we live in very **different worlds.**

Under the Influence

You loved me in your drunkenness,
but it didn't transfer over to your sobriety.

Was I just a part of your addiction,
while you were the entirety of
of mine?

Real life irony made into bittersweet poetry.

I never tasted a drop of anything but you;
and yet I loved you like I was completely intoxicated.

I guess in the end, we're all **under the influence** of
something...

or someone.

Caged In

My heart is so heavy tonight that if my ribs weren't keeping it caged in,

I would

Collapse

under its weight.

Lost at Sea (In My Soul)

Do you ever feel the waves of trauma rippling through
your body because they have nowhere else to go?
Nowhere to run, nowhere to hide.
The turbulent tide that constantly resides, flooding your
heart and sinking your mind.
Is it just me? Surely it can't be.
This weight of the ocean crashing internally; a sea layered
deep in anxiety. There's no escaping from what's within.
Under the water it's so well hidden. The current in motion
forms a hurricane of violent emotions, while stirring up
memories of everything I know.
It ebbs and flows, this violent undertow.
Never showing on the surface, but swallows me whole
from the pressure below. I surrender once more to the
unforgiving power that's taken such a sad toll,
and quietly drown another death from inside the depths of
my own submerged soul.

Fighting the Familiar

Sometimes I hate myself for even thinking of you.
For letting my heart run to the familiar place where you live inside my mind. I don't even want you there, but the memories feed you and keep you alive.

I haven't figured out if I'm comforting the demons when I visit…

Or if they're comforting me.

Rhythmic Release

It's 3am now.
I'm seeing red.
Thoughts of you swirl viciously inside my head.
All the memories unrelenting,
pulsating in my skull.
Sending waves of energy to my chest,
pumping hard as the blood pools.
Deep thumps in my ribs and
erratic breaths now.
My heart and mind are booming from the inside.
So loud I can hear it, both inside and out of my mind
(and I am out of my mind).
The reverberated heartbeat sound.
I will explode if I don't calm down.
I start to cry and write all the things my body is dying to
(but can only silently) shout.
Releasing some of the pressure,
hoping for some relief as the pain rhythmically pours out.

Love's Logic

Maybe the reason broken hearts feel so damn heavy is because there are so many shattered pieces. Logically it makes no sense, but in matters of love and loss, we rarely think rationally anyway. So I continue to tell myself this in hopes that there is some purpose in eventually putting it back together again...

That one day the weight of a scarred, but whole heart, will be lighter to carry.

Bittersweet Release

Will my love ever be enough to soften the outer edges of your rigid heart?

My fingers are raw from holding on so long. You give just enough hope to keep me holding on.

But the harder I love you, the more I just continue to bleed. I'm ready to let you go…

But
you'll never fully release your grip
on me.

Truth Dipped in Poison

You wrapped me up in a false sense of security.
Held me hostage to your beautiful lies.
You tasted of sweet deception,
but there were hints of honesty hidden in your eyes.

Love and betrayal interlaced,
truth dipped in poison
leaves a bittersweet aftertaste.
A toxic swirl of contradiction
when reality and fiction get misplaced.

Ripped Open

I tried so hard to protect your heart at all costs.
Holding it together while my own drowned in the chaos.
I'm setting you free so that you don't sink with me.
My burdensome dead weight you don't need to carry.
Please don't think this is easy.
You deserve so much more than I can give.
It sounds cliché, but the guilt still stings.
My wrists are tied and rope burned from fighting truth's inevitable strings.
It wasn't fair to keep you trapped inside of a box.
I had to set healing boundaries for us both,
but I guess in the end we both lost.
Backfired words meant with only love in mind,
have now **ripped open** this already scarred heart of mine.

Lying Lullabies

My soul is so unsettled and my heart is filled with overwhelming unrest. Some nights I just can't sing the demons back to sleep.

These lullabies, how pathologically they lie. And no matter how many words I find, none of them fall into the formation that leads to a happy ending in this bedtime story relentlessly raging in my mind.

There's no chance of sleep so instead I write, but even fully awake, I can't edit myself out of this living nightmare tonight.

Suicide Love

By now, I must have mourned for you a hundred different times. Although in reality, you've never really died. So many of your emotional deaths I've had to endure, as I continually outlive this trauma-cycle ride. You repeatedly chose to love and leave; dying to me a little more each time. This ongoing sadness breaks my heart and I suffer with grief inside. I tried so hard to keep this love of ours alive, but after all this time the truth is there's nothing left here to revive. It wasn't just that our love had died...

Mine fought to survive, while yours committed *suicide.*

Love

Rising Above Reason

Sometimes
when we lift others up,
they invite us to fly with them.
Rising above,
beyond all reason,
we're carried on the wings
of *love.*

Written Between Our Souls

The best poetry is
written with eye contact between two souls.
Magnetic telepathy
that just naturally flows.
Together we write
the most beautiful **love poems**
that no one will ever read.
Your **heart** and my **soul**
hold all the **magic** we'll ever need.

Chamber Walls

Within these walls,
in the chamber of my heart
you've taken hold
staked your claim
found a home and
flooded every part.
Overflowed it with love
filling every scarred place.
These words you speak
directly and relentlessly
echo in this sacred space.
They surround my soul
falling gently on my skin,
like soft raindrops
quenching me from within.
With every spoken word
you grip me intimately,
as I let you in my world
I feel you so emotionally.
And I freely surrender
all of me
to you...

Unapologetically.

All Things Warm

Prophetically you found me…
Lonely and cold, without a spark.
I was so lost without the sunlight,
A forced worshiper of the dark.
But I feel your warmth between all the pages,
like dawn breaking through the darkest of ages.
Your light heals my soul, and shines regardless of the season.
I write of you effortlessly without needing a reason.
You're making me a believer
In all things warm…
Painting pictures of sunsets,
and being the calm in my storm.

Everything

It's that real deal
Heart stopping
Soul gripping
Dancing in the kitchen
Kissing in the rain
Wear his T-shirt all day
Missed the whole movie
(but not even complaining)
Lost in his eyes
Under the stars
Finding true north
Every song singing
Love note leaving
Held under the covers
In his arms
Never gets old
Guiding light
Where I belong
Once in this lifetime
And every past life before
Finally home feeling
Safe and sound
Now whole
True love's counterpart
Lost in love,
Deep in my soul,
Written on my heart...
Forever kind of thing.

Kiss me like there's no tomorrow...

Because even forever with you will never be enough.

Poetic Love

Poetic love is the most dangerous of all.

Yet here we all are risking the fall.

Pens in our steady hands,
hearts on sleeves displayed for all to see.
Walking on love's ledge, souls exposed and intertwined, as words dangle off the paper's edge.

It bleeds across pages that outlast every broken heart. Poems that outlive every twin flame's fire with unmatched desire even when we fall apart.

We write cathartic messages from deep inside our very bones, and inscribe words upon eternity for healing, even when it's not our own.

Yes, poetic love is often reckless, precarious, and crazy indeed...

Yet we all keep pouring it out, in hopes to fill the scars that still continue to bleed.

Timeless Love

I love you in ways I don't even fully understand,
from places I can't always recall,
in depths that can't be measured,
as you break down my every wall.

I see you in every lifetime,
as my soul is naturally drawn to yours.
You're the voice behind these words of mine,
and it's so far beyond coincidental.

You tip-toe through my past life memories and leave a trail
of sprinkled stardust mixed with familiar smiles behind.
The universal guiding light that always leads me to what I'm
meant to find.

Our love weaves seamlessly through different centuries,
perhaps even galaxies or beyond.
You're the hero from my dreams, my gravitational force
with a one way pull, it seems.

And no amount of time or space can ever break these star
aligned synchronicities.

I'm deeply in love with you.

Body
Mind
Soul

It's that simple.

But also...

That complicated

Wrapped Up In Your Love

I want to gaze at the stars while being wrapped in your arms.
Feel your kisses on my forehead, as our
fingers interlace.
Let the sound of your heartbeat lull me to sleep on your chest.
We'll wake up in time to catch the sunrise,
while being trapped beneath blankets with
magic still in your eyes.
Breathing you in like oxygen.
Yesterdays fade into tomorrows.
All sense of time is lost,
in this fantasy turned reality.
You and me together in this
Heaven kissed anomaly.

Light In My Darkness

You pulled me in like I was the moon,
and still loved me in my darkest of phases.

You must be the sun, because when I look at you all I do is
reflect light in the darkest of places.

No Place Like Home

You found yourself
in my heart again,
as I got lost in your eyes.
Reunited after parting ways,
temporarily separated,
and in need of a little space.
We fell headfirst into sweet familiarity,
as time generously held our place.
The past resurrected, healed, and cleansed,
in a beautiful transformation.
Our house of bookmarked memories now turned into our
homecoming celebration.
The door was open,
the lights were on
and we walked right in.
Your arms are like fate,
I feel so safe with you,
and it feels so good
to finally be home again.

Uninterrupted Space

I'm so tired of loving you with restraint.

Take me to that place of uninterrupted space.

Unlimited access to your soul;

heart to heart,

and face to face.

Where I'm finally able to breathe in all of you,

and no longer suffocating in your embrace.

Love is the only trap
That sets your heart free...

And I promise you,
I've thrown away every single key.

Reflections in Ink

You and I bleed from the same pen.
Words interwoven, reflecting from within.
Souls intertwined from long long ago;
perhaps another space and time.
You speak to my heart
and see beyond my mind.
When my soul shines through
It's a mirror of sorts,
ricocheting my thoughts as my words mix with yours.
We write to breathe,
and so the story goes,
when it comes to you and me,
the ink between us just effortlessly flows.

Electricity

Love me like a thunderstorm,
in the rushing of winds
and in torrential pouring rain.
Wrap me in a blizzard of ecstasy;
a windblown mess,
a swirling hurricane.
Shock me with the voltage
of lightning across the sky.
This bolt of energy connecting us;
the electricity between
you and I.

Embedded

The love I have for you
is woven deep into my bones,
and knitted within the core of my soul.
There's no way of releasing it,
despite wanting to let it go.
I can't escape from what has become a permanent piece of
me now, although we're so far apart.
Even long after we've parted ways,
you'll forever be embedded in my blood,
and always rooted
in my heart.

YOU

The truth is you're the first thing I think of when I wake up each day.

You're on my mind all the time.
Everything makes me think of you. It's the little insignificant things that trigger memories and thoughts. The way the sunlight sneaks in through the window on a brisk fall morning and I'm reminded of your warmth. The song I hear and start to wonder how someone knew exactly what was singing in my heart for you. The excitement of hoping to share the future together. Funny stupid things that only we know about. I catch myself smiling for no reason and then realize it's because of you. Always you. I look forward to every moment we get to spend together and miss you whenever we're apart. You can piss me off so easily, and then in the same moment make me laugh so effortlessly that I forget what I was even mad about. Perhaps it's because I'm madly in love with every little thing about you, now and forever. Your flaws, your voice, your smile.
Everything imperfect.
It will always be you.

Healing & Soul Lessons

I'm healing.

But damn,

it still hurts.

Shadow Work

Midnight strolls down the path

of raw vulnerability.

The soul exposed in all of its fragility.

There in the moonlight,

so much truth is revealed.

By dawn's sunrise,

so much can be healed.

Saving Ourselves

Most of us don't need anyone to save us.

If anything...

We need to be loved in broken pieces,

while we put them back together,

becoming whole,

as we save ourselves.

Undone

I feel myself coming undone.
Unraveling in sweet release.
Shedding what's no longer needed.
Laying false notions to rest.
Seeking solace for my soul.
Letting go and trusting that all things will land
exactly where they're meant to fall.

Holding it together
makes people think you're so strong.
But in reality there's so much power in letting go,
of all that needs to be undone.

Anomaly

Who would have known the anomaly that would become of me?
From seeds of doubt sown deep into my soul, planting toxicity.
Deliberately trying to destroy me from within while inflicting so much hurt.
Rooted in heartbreak and buried in sorrow.
My trampled heart; good as dead in the dirt.
Somehow I found a way to survive on faith, tears, and sunlight. From ashes of despair sprouted courage and strength; blooming into something uncontainable and beautifully bright.
For you see, I am no longer writing as the girl who needs to be rescued…
But instead as the woman who saved herself.

Brighter Days

My light feels like it's growing dim,
but it will never completely fade away.
I'm lost in the maze of my own mind these days,
but my heart will never wander astray.
I fall into the darkness that has become like a home.
A mere silhouette of my spirit clothed in gentle monochrome.
My thoughts are so deep, that most would drown (and many already have).
I'm almost out of breath,
but my words are forever penned in stone.
My intuition lights the way,
when I can't see beyond the haze.
This inner glow, forever shining
that will soon light the path
toward my own brighter days.

The Light Within

I smiled through my tears for so many years;
watering down my sadness in an attempt to grow
happiness.
We all wear our scars in camouflaged ways,
to hide the shame and deny the pain.
Survival looks different from day to day;
as we need the sunlight to balance the rain.
The moon has the power to control the tides,
but it takes work in the shadows to heal hearts and mend
minds.
Looking for warmth when the darkness looms,
is like hoping for fake flowers to magically bloom.
The change never happens in just one night.
We ebb and we flow, and slowly we grow.
Trusting that one day we will look within,
and finally be able to see
our own light.

Peace Amongst Demons

When you left
I made peace with the demons
that lived inside my mind.

They're not so bad and it seems your absence has rendered
them somewhat kind.

I thought I had lost everything,
but it turns out you were never really mine to find.

The Calm In My Storm

You didn't come rushing in like sunshine during a storm.
Instead you saw my chaos and sat with me in the rain.
We listened to the thunder and felt the pain.
We slept under clouds until the fog rolled away.
We felt so much more than words could ever say.
You weren't the sun, but your soul felt warm.
You were the exact calm I needed in the middle of my life's turbulent storm.

Growing Pains

It's incredible how many ways we grow from pain.

The poison and remedy are often different shades of the same color gray.

Love often leads to heartbreak and
heartbreak is healed by love...

In this never ending cycle of lessons we're all part of.

The Space Between

If words were enough,
I would have saved us both.
I spoke life into your barely beating heart,
but you soon grew tone deaf to my voice.
You stopped listening when I would speak,
and now all I can do is sit and think.
The silence expanded the space between.

Now, instead I pour it all out through a pen.
Healing words once left for dead.
You'll never hear my voice,
see my heart, or truly know the depths of my soul,
but my heart will forever bleed between pages that you'll never read...

But so many others will.

Gone

I had to cut you out like a cancer this time to finally save myself...

Every last piece
Premeditated
Carved out
Methodically lacerated
Separated
Washed clean
Mentally amputated
Nothing left
Physically terminated
Emotionally sedated
Vanished without a trace
Memory erased
Mind manipulated
Soul emaciated
Pain induced
Feelings reduced
Permanently removed
Numbed strife
Emotions transplanted
Love's sacrifice
Logic's knife
Loss of limb to
Spare my life

Weeds and Wishes

You left such a deep hole in my heart, that all I could do was turn it into a flower bed hoping to make something beautiful out of the void.

But sometimes seeds of doubt
still grow
and stems of worry
start to sprout.
Between my ribs
they find their way out.

But weeds can still be wishes
as this grave became a garden.
Watered with my tears,
bringing seeds into full bloom.
Filling spaces left by by fears and
planting life in places previously filled with doom.

Seasons change and many things die
but spring comes around and dead things may rise.
It's proof that you can reap beautiful things
from sadness that was once sown.
Even headstones are adorned with flowers
as we remember those we miss...
And cemeteries holding eternal death
are often overgrown with beauty on the surface.

Shaped Soul

Like a river rock
tumbling through the stream,
I journey through each life lesson
slowly softening.
Every turn shapes my soul
rounding me out
smoothing me down
while refining my edges and
making me whole.
From the outside in
these rushing waters heal me,
keeping me grounded
while also setting me free.

Spiritual Journey

My soul has awakened,
and now other parts of me must die.
My heart halts to a standstill
as my mind races against the clock of fictitious reality.
Truly time is just an illusion,
but we get stuck in its gravity.
Pulling us away from the divine healing source found inside
of all of us spiritually.
We're merely souls on spiritual voyages
in these bodies as vessels, physically.
Eventually we'll raise our vibration and travel toward the
light, at a higher frequency.

Still Alive

I felt my heart sink as I closed the door.
You wanted parts of me, but nothing more.

I settled for so long,
paying heartbreak's toll.
You killed my spirit
and scarred my soul.

I'm so far from whole,
with discarded pieces I hope to **_revive_**.
My heart is barely beating,
But it's proof that my weary soul
is somehow still beautifully **_alive_**.

I will survive.

Caged

Isn't it ironic
the way
we can feel both safe
and enslaved
within the exact
same cage?

Dead End

To hell with letting myself wander down that road again.

The one filled with red flags and hazard signs at every stop.

That bumpy, unpaved, crooked road with dangerous twists

and turns around every single bend.

That road that's nothing but a trap leading straight to you…

A dead end.

I'll follow my heart far into the unknown.

Somewhere with magical light glowing ahead.

Poetry and Pain

Which came first, the poetry or the pain?
Sunshine or rain?
Love or heartbreak?
Acceptance or blame?
Thoughts I can't contain.
Words now ink stains.
Beautifully spilled.
Keeping me sane.
Bled onto pages
as cathartic remains.

Held

I'm tough as hell,
But sometimes...

I just need to be held.

Love and Logic

Actions speak louder than words…

It's true.

And right now both of yours are so quiet
that emptiness floods your eyes.
Everything echos narcissism
and silently screams of lies.

I found my way back into this mess of you,
overlooking so many warning signs.
Now, I'll fight like hell to crawl my way out,
even if it means crossing back over love and logic's
permanent lines.

Lost in Translation

I get lost in translation
between love and a broken heart.
That's the reason I'm either smiling
or falling apart.
There is no in between, it's all or nothing it seems.
I'm either stuck in a nightmare,
or trying to daydream.

Enslaved, But Saved

You might have imprisoned my heart

But in doing so,

you set all my words free.

Thank you for the lesson

that will ultimately

heal me.

The Ocean In My Bones

I carry the weight of the ocean in my bones.

And I feel as though my strength is draining as the waters rise; hidden parts of me full of demise.

My soul is saturated with salt water,
and emotional currents roar inside my mind.
Ripples of remorse fill my heart,
now surrendered and overpowered.

The tide rushes in and floods me with
all the things I've already cast out,
attempting to drown me once again beneath the waves of regret and doubt.

The water stings as salt seeps into my unhealed scars. I can barely breathe and my wounds now burn.
It swallows me whole and then launches me back to the shore, completely undone, but cleansed from within.

The same sea I was sinking in has saved me from myself. From a raging storm to a healing rain, the water soothes my thirsty soul, and washes away the pain. I'm poured back together, mixed with love and forgiveness, and my ocean deep soul is finally at peace once again.

Free To Fly

You cradled my soul like a fragile baby bird
so carefully in your strong but gentle hands.
You patiently waited until I was ready,
helped me spread my wings,
and watched
as I finally began to *fly*.

Layered In Light

Casting shadows
On the edge of darkness
Falling through trauma cycles
Landing in pools of self-reflection
Drowning in deep soul convictions
Wading through heartache
Submerged in pain
Buried in doubt
Cleansed in spiritual rain
Found in grace
Rescued with hope
Awakened to intuition
Embodied with wisdom
Healed with love
Layered in light

Keeper Of Darkness

I weave words through injured souls like spiritual sutures.
Healing hearts and mending minds.
Love pours down like rain.
Sewing threads of lightning through thunderclouds.
Helping the wounded find their light through the pain.

Even if it means I must hold on to their darkness long after the storm passes, so they can finally see the sun again.

Unbreakable

My soul is unbreakable...

But that doesn't mean parts of it aren't in need of

healing.

Set Free

Let it all just crumble
to the ground
Every tiny part
Every last piece
Burned down
Scattered about
Completely lost
All the evidence
Faded away
No matter
the cost
Undone
Empty
No more you...
Just me
now healed
and finally set free

Writing Myself Well

When the night is finally quiet, and peace temporarily blankets every last corner of my home. When all the children have drifted off and the world seems to finally stand still. No one needs anything, and I'm reminded of the simple desires woven into my weary soul. This sacred time comes where rest is vital, but the countdown to the dawn's next day's monotony is inevitable. This cherished moment of grace, giving my mind the hallowed space of needed respite in this silent place. Sleep is the goal, but writing is my reward. A bittersweet paradox of the sickness and the cure. A cost I can't really afford, but is altogether priceless if not ignored. I feel the rush of a thousand words flooding through my veins. My mind is plagued with relentless thoughts battling inside my brain. I'll choke on the verbiage if I don't breathe it into life. Built up, tongue-tied, cut open, spilled over and set free, thanks to the pen that doubles as my knife. The time gave me way more than it took, and I'll find evidence of restoration in the morning nestled between the healing pages of my soul's beloved book.

Written Rampage

Is mental illness contagious?

Or more like a cancer in its various stages?

Thoughts like birds confined to cages,

trapped in a mind that constantly rages.

Madness poured out in written rampages.

Crazy emotions spilled onto pages.

The price is sanity paid as wages.

The ink is the hostage of imprisoned outrages.

Bittersweet truth left stained for all of the ages.

Hungry For Love

I'm so sorry for the version of myself I was back then. The damaged me you came to know. You weren't perfect either, and at the time my heart was so far from well.

I was starved emotionally to the point of eating your lies, and actually convinced myself they tasted good. Bittersweet half truths washed down with occasional tears made for a slow poisoning of the soul.

Hungry for love, but instead I settled for your empty caloric lust. I was blinded at first, but I soon came to fully understand. I was misused, but not confused. Trapped, but still at home in your heart of constant contradictions. I rendered myself comforted amongst the complacency.

It held me over for a while, but I couldn't lie to myself nearly as well as you could. You were the best at making me doubt everything about who I was. You made it clear that I was too much and simultaneously never enough. In reality you had your own voids you tried to fill with my pieces, but never wanted all that I was capable of.

You handed me the shovel, but I was the one digging my own grave the whole time. Tossing in the parts you didn't want. Slowly dying, pieces at a time.

It's so sad how a starving soul will devour deception like a delicacy when it thinks there is nothing else to satisfy the hunger inside.

But fortunately, I'm made with indestructible fibers of generational strength that wouldn't let those emaciated parts die without having a second chance. I rose from the figurative grave, redesigned with a transformed heart, soul, and mind.

I guess it's true what they say about coal transforming into diamonds when buried under enough immense pressure. They're as hard as the hell they've been through, and will eventually shine beyond all measure.

The grave I started still remains. It's used specifically for thoughts of you in an emotionally bulimic type of way. At first taste, I heave you up and into the ground so that one day you'll be completely gone, and never again to be found.

Thank you

I want to thank you for leaving me stranded and alone in the dark.

It forced me down a path in search of light,

and in the process I found my way back to the fire within my own heart.

Wholly Healing

May my heart grow fierce.

May my mind find peace.

May my spirit fly free.

May my body grow in strength.

May my soul align with divine source.

Strengthening My Soul

Soaring with angels
Strengthening my soul with light
Spirit flying free

Written Remedy

I'm so messed up,
that I don't even want to write tonight.
Afraid of what might spill out of my pen.
The usual battle I often fight.
But I've been here before and I know the means to this story's end.
Write out my messy chaotic heart.
Not if, but when.
It's the pills I don't take and the liquids I don't drink.
I write to numb the pain,
but also simultaneously feel the sting.
It's masochistic therapy;
the only wound that heals faster the more it bleeds,
this addiction to ***writing myself well***.
It's the cure that helps, but also hurts;
as I write out the remedy like a self-help inner love spell.

Inner Work

Healing often takes place in the silence between our deepest and most shallow breaths. We quietly bind up wounds people don't even see, and resolve hidden traumas we don't always understand. This inner work is done within the hushed trenches of our sacred souls. The tiniest teardrops sometimes escape as pain is released, but most often, to others, it's completely unknown. Shadow work growth, that is uniquely our own. Rarely spilled out, or never shown. Sometimes progress can only be measured by surviving one fragile moment to the next. Our hurt will eventually lessen as we seek to understand the beauty hidden in the lesson.

Never Will Be

It's true.
There are two sides to every story
And you...
You've become my own personal
life lesson allegory.
Teaching me all the things
I wish I didn't have to know.
It's the hard way of learning
and of constantly letting go.
Pruning away pieces of you so that I can hopefully grow.
I keep chasing after things that aren't meant for me.
You were never mine and no matter how hard I try,
You ***never will be***.

Lightworkers

It's true...
They walk among us.

Or rather,
we exist among you.

Endless wanderers.
The ones with souls deeper than the ocean.

Magical healers.
The ones with hearts full of holes where light now pierces through.

Loyal protectors.
The ones who fight silent battles with warrior spirits.

Us.
The ones born in the darkness only to be transformed into workers of the light.

No One Believed Me

They thought I had nothing to say.

Little did they know my mind is a fortress built with remnants of a broken heart.

The pieces are strong as Hell, mended from Heaven,

leaving my soul a tapestry of magical parts.

AT THE END OF THE DAY I PRAY MY HEART SPILLS OUT INTO THE SHAPE OF A BEAUTIFUL SOUL.

Crossroad

And then one day everything changed.

I woke up on the other side of the collateral damage.

This unfamiliar crossroad, beyond all the wreckage.

Somewhere between being wounded and healed.

Between a bleeding heart and healed scars.

Between past pain and new numbness.

Beyond the war zone, but not quite yet home.

Much farther away from my once broken heart, but amidst the valley of the curious and unknown.

As I meander through the depths of my own beautifully chaotic mind, I'm a **soulful wanderer**, never sure of what I'll find.

Uncharted territory…
But no longer trapped behind enemy lines.

Beautiful Darkness

Like caterpillars that fall into a deep sleep,
sometimes we too are in need of stepping away from the outside world and trusting in the unknown. Wisdom grows within the shadows of our own mysterious slumber. Falling into solitude, we step away to give our souls a quiet space to rest and grow; a peaceful place for our hearts to heal.
Once the metamorphosis is complete, the light finally breaks through and we see what we've become. A beautiful butterfly with a magical glow.
We remember the darkness with nothing but gratitude, for that is where our intuition led us.
The place where wings of fate could finally grow.

Don't Get Me Wrong

I am ready for this heartache to end.
But as long as I'm hurting,
the truth keeps pouring out of this pen.
Words drip out in a poetic mess.
Cathartically written from trauma regressed.
My heart starts to heal and emotions spill, resulting in ink-stained chaos.
Eventually my tears will wash away all the pain,
but thankfully the beauty of this lesson
will always remain.

Misaligned

What can be written
that hasn't already been said?
Was it just a drop in time among us?
Or my starving soul literally dying to be fed?
It feels like an ocean between what was once alive,
and is now dead.
I keep fighting for you from inside the wounded
part of my mind.
This hold you have on my heart,
keeps my soul from being fully aligned.
I'm done being held hostage to your unreciprocated love
in this war game I'll never win.
I'm stitching up what's left of my scarred heart,
and setting myself free from this prison you've kept me in.

Submerged in Self-Reflection

My soul is deeper than the ocean, and while so many have tried to swim across in vain, tonight I'm the one navigating in the depths of my own shadowed pain. There's work to be done where the light doesn't reach. So much inner healing needs to take place and self-reflection from this lonely beach. Waves of tears wash over me entirely, as I drown myself in the harsh truth, seeking clarity. I'm holding all this weight that I no longer need to carry. All the parts you can't see until you dive beneath the surface. I let myself sink to the bottom of the sea, learn the lesson, let it go, leaving it on the ocean floor, and finally forgive the ugliest parts of me.

War Zone

Someday my heart and mind will fight for me from the same side of the war.

Love and logic, no longer enemies...

And there won't be such a paradox of what they're fighting for.

Crying Words

When I can't cry,
words become my tears.
Falling onto pages,
all these hopes and fears.
Sobbing silently,
landing letter by letter,
cathartically.
While my heart quietly hurts inside,
I let the floodwaters wash over paper
from deep inside my mind.
I release my emotions like caged birds.
I write because life doesn't always have time for tears,
and also to help heal those who can read
but don't know yet
how to cry words.

Wishing You Well

After it all,
I still wish you well.
You broke my heart so easily,
but I was the one who willingly fell.

Needed Most

We don't talk...

But there's stuff my heart still wants you to know.

I want you to know that my thoughts always find their way back to you,
no matter how hard I try to lose myself in everything and anything else.

It's in the quietness of my mind that we are now at **peace**,
even though I'm here all alone with just shadows of your ghost.

I wanted your love back,
but what I needed was
healing
the most.

Finally Free

Set me free today
In both truth and in action.
Set me free this time,
full of strength and conviction.
Set me free at last,
filled with steadfast devotion.
Set me free for good,
never returning to this state of mind.
Set me free from you,
and let me be
just me,
finally free.

Feeling The Fall

The winds of change blew golden rays straight into her gypsy heart, stirring all the magic from within her old soul. As the trees began to change and the leaves started to fall, she too felt that same beautiful release of letting dead things go. It's funny how losing some lifeless parts heal you from the inside and make you feel whole. She felt all the pieces start to finally align, and as the autumn moonlight danced across her face, she knew that this was her time to shine.

Unfolded

I thought I knew what love was.

But as it turns out, I think life is just one big lesson where I keep an ongoing list of what it's not. I suppose it's different for everyone. Trial and error, success and failure. Always learning, moving, growing, expanding. Perhaps as we evolve towards our highest good, so does our concept of love. As we emerge into the most authentic version of who we're meant to be, so does our perception of the love we have for others, and perhaps more importantly, for ourselves. We gather pieces of wisdom along this journey, little parts becoming whole. It's like layers of darkness unfolding until we can finally see the light that was always shining from deep within our soul.

Breaking to Become

Breaking one's heart can awaken the soul.

Life lessons learned in pieces,

eventually making you **whole**.

Seeds of Hope

I never thought I'd say this, but the lesson learned was worth all the hurt and heartache I endured.

I see my beautiful battle scars formed from such deep wounds, and I'm reminded of how far I've come and how much more I will continue to bloom.

Behind these bruises are seeds of hope.
They may be watered with tears,
but it's how I cope.
Every bit of growth is worth the fight.

Adding self love to my soul for healing light .

Aligned

Sometimes the only type of rest you need is the kind when you distance your heart from your mind so your soul can be at peace.

Apart, but **aligned**.

Separate energies all balanced.

Powerful beyond measure when finally **combined**.

Meant to Stay

I've learned to take things in moments,
day by day.

Also,
that a lot of things come along,
but only some
are meant to stay.

Home

At the end of the day,
all I want to know
is that my intuition lit the path
for my soul to find its way home.

More

This mind of mine, it never stops.

Maybe it's running from reality.
Or perhaps,
always chasing dreams.

Either way,
it knows there's so much more to this life...

Than what it seems.

Forget

When it comes to certain things,
I just try to forget.
They're not worth remembering.
Not even as regrets.

Worlds Apart

How could I expect

you to see that I was dying,

when we feel so differently

about what it means

to truly

feel

alive?

Sacred Sounds

Searching
for silence amongst all the noise.
Drowning out everything
and tuning into my own inner voice.
My body, mind, and soul align from within.
Sacred sounds of truth whisper to my heart
of inner healing, wisdom,
and
spiritual
intuition.

The Hope

As children,
we were taught to be kind to others.

As adults,
we need constant reminders to be kind to ourselves.

The hope
is that someday
we'll learn how to do
both.

> *Unapologetically unavailable to anyone or anything that doesn't align with reaching my soul's highest good at the moment.*
>
> ♥

Learning to Listen

I think the universe has been speaking to me

(and you too)

my whole life,

but I'm just now learning

to value when it's silent so I can

listen.

The Journey

The journey back to your self can be a treacherous and painful one.

However, reaching the ***final destination of your own heart*** is worth all the lessons learned along the way.

Leaving Us Raw

The truth has a way

of pruning away

all of the things

that no longer serve us,

leaving us raw

with authenticity

and ready for true growth.

Wrong and Right

Sometimes

sharing your soul

with the wrong person

can teach you

all of the

right lessons.

Some of Us

Some of us feel things that can't be seen.

We listen beyond the lyrics,

heal our wounds with magical words,

and suture our souls between songs.

We tune into frequencies

and ground into Earth's energies.

We seek the sun,

and soak in its healing light.

We manifest new destinies

under the glow of the moon at night.

We dream while wide awake,

and trust in the unknown.

We break generational trauma cycles,

follow our intuition...

and find lessons carved out of heartbreak.

Lifetimes of Lessons

She was too magical to settle for the mundane, even though she was only just beginning to understand her own magic.

She carried hundreds of stories hidden within her heart from many lifetimes of lessons learned. And although she didn't win every battle, the curses broken were worth every scar she earned.

For so long she walked in darkness, not realizing that light was escaping from the cracks in her heart.

She was shining light and illuminating the path to help those around her find their way out of their own shadows.

The Shift

I'm shifting my focus

and rewiring my mind.

Seeking my purpose,

not sure of what I'll find.

Changing perspectives

and opening up to endless possibilities.

Finding the good,

and defying prewritten destinies.

Born Into Darkness

Children of the light are so often born into darkness.

And as they grow they learn how to glow.

This journey is one of karmic purposes.

They ignite sparks as a way of survival to guide their way,

leaving an illuminated path to love's source for all others to follow.

The Way Home

So many lost souls

wandering through lifetimes

hoping to find the golden ticket

to their final destination,

not realizing the purpose in the journey

will lead them back home

straight into their very own hearts.

Warrior Spirit

She felt the whole of Earth's energy shift.

An awakening that can't be explained with words.

A truly indescribable feeling only some of us can sense.

The day she realized she had to stop trying to save the world, and instead truly save herself first.

She redirected the focus of worldly battles to the unrelenting spiritual war deep within her own soul.

She then rose up and conquered giants inside herself which rippled into helping decimate the fear of those around her.

Her power spoke for itself. She didn't fully understand it, but she trusted it completely.

With unshakable faith, and a contagious warrior spirit, she used her life to empower others to do the same and ended up helping the world heal in greater ways than she ever dreamed of.

...My Dear Sweet Child...
A Poem written in 1987 by My Dad,
Barry Weaver

May you never fear to dream,
or to hold what you can't touch.
For everything is within your reach,
when your passion is high enough.
So as you grow with passing days,
becoming older all the time,
may all your castles, queens, and dreams,
live within the locket of your mind.
Your eyes are as bright as sunshine,
even when you cry.
Your smile is more explosive,
than fireworks in July.
You will always have my prayers,
I'll say them everyday.
Much like silent tears,
they will never fade away.
I wish I had your youth,
your innocence, and your size,
to see the world as you do,
through the windows of your eyes.

I found the power in using
my voice,
but now I'm mastering the
magic
that dwells in the silence
of my soul.

With so much love,
Samantha

"The part you play on the world's stage is determined by your conception of yourself. By feeling your wish fulfilled and quietly relaxing into sleep, you cast yourself in a star role to be played on earth tomorrow, and, while asleep, you are rehearsed and instructed in your part."

Neville Goddard

ABOUT THE AUTHOR

Samantha is a wife, mom, teacher, and homeless youth coordinator. She is a California native, but lived in Hawaii for a few short years. She lives with her awesome husband and two crazy, amazing children, and many animals. She's easily distracted by the sky, loves the ocean, and wants to adopt all the animals.

She holds a bachelor's degree in Liberal Arts, a Multiple Subject Teaching Credential in the state of California, and a master's degree in Education.

She released her first book, **Words of a Feather** on 2/22/22, but was already deep into writing this one. Both can be found on Amazon.

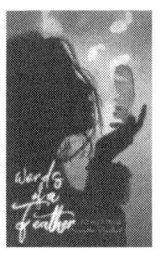

You can find more of her work on Instagram and Facebook @Soul_Spilled_Sentiments

Printed in Great Britain
by Amazon